BABY MAMMOTH MUMMY

FROZEN IN TIME!

BABY MAMMOTH MUMMY

FROZEN IN TIME!

A PREHISTORIC ANIMAL'S JOURNEY INTO THE 21ST CENTURY

BY CHRISTOPHER SLOAN

WITH THE GENEROUS COOPERATION OF BERNARD BUIGUES

PHOTOGRAPHY BY FRANCIS LATREILLE

NATIONAL GEOGRAPHIC

WASHINGTON, D.C.

PUBLISHED BY THE NATIONAL GEOGRAPHIC SOCIETY

John M. Fahey, Jr., *Chairman of the Board and Chief Executive Officer*
Tim T. Kelly, *President*
Declan Moore, *Executive Vice President; President, Publishing*
Melina Gerosa Bellows, *Executive Vice President; Chief Creative Officer, Books, Kids, and Family*

PREPARED BY THE BOOK DIVISION

Nancy Laties Feresten, *Senior Vice President, Editor in Chief, Children's Books;* Jonathan Halling, *Design Director, Books and Children's Publishing;* Jay Sumner, *Director of Photography, Children's Publishing;* Jennifer Emmett, *Editorial Director, Children's Books;* Carl Mehler, *Director of Maps;* R. Gary Colbert, *Production Director;* Jennifer A. Thornton, *Managing Editor*

STAFF FOR THIS BOOK

Robin Terry, *Project Editor;* Suzanne Patrick Fonda, *Editor;* James Hiscott, Jr., *Art Director/Designer;* Lori Epstein, *Senior Illustrations Editor;* Kate Olesin, *Editorial Assistant;* Kathryn Robbins, *Design Production Assistant;* Hillary Moloney, *Illustrations Assistant;* Gregory Ugiansky, *Map Production;* Grace Hill, *Associate Managing Editor;* Lewis R. Bassford, *Production Manager;* Susan Borke, *Legal and Business Affairs*

MANUFACTURING AND QUALITY MANAGEMENT

Christopher A. Liedel, *Chief Financial Officer;* Phillip L. Schlosser, *Senior Vice President;* Chris Brown, *Technical Director;* Rachel Faulise, Nicole Elliot, and Robert L. Barr, *Managers*

Library of Congress Cataloging-in-Publication Data

Sloan, Christopher.
Baby mammoth mummy : frozen in time : a prehistoric animal's journey into the 21st century / by Chris Sloan.
    p. cm.
Includes bibliographical references and index.
ISBN 978-1-4263-0865-9 (hardcover : alk. paper)—
ISBN 978-1-4263-0866-6 (lib. bdg. : alk. paper)
1. Mammoths—Russia (Federation)—Siberia—Juvenile literature. 2. Paleontology—Pleistocene—Juvenile literature. I. Title.
QE882.P8S56 2011
569'.670957—dc22
                            2010044003
Printed in U.S.A.
11/WOR/1

FOR OLIVER, IOLA, AND LEIF

ACKNOWLEDGMENTS

This book is the result of the labors of many people, all of whom I thank for making it possible. I have special thanks for Bernard Buigues for his support of this project and Dan Fisher, who spent hours answering questions and helping to make this book as accurate as possible. I'd also like to thank David Fox and Adam Rountrey for reading the text and reviewing the graphics for accuracy.

ILLUSTRATION CREDITS

All photographs by Francis Latreille unless otherwise noted below:

10, Bernard Buigues; 16, Stuart Armstrong; 17, Karel Havlicek/NationalGeographic Stock.com; 28 (lo), Naoki Suzuki/NationalGeographicStock.com; 29, Kazuhiko Sano/ NationalGeographicStock.com; 30, Kazuhiko Sano/NationalGeographicStock.com; 31 (lo), Hannes Grobe; 32 (lo le), Lida Xing/NationalGeographicStock.com; 32 (lo rt), Kennis & Kennis/NationalGeographicStock.com; 32 (up), John Gurche/National GeographicStock.com; 33 (up le), Gregory Manchess/NationalGeographicStock.com; 33 (up rt), Gregory A. Harlin/NationalGeographicStock.com; 33 (lo), Stuart Armstrong; 34–35, Mauricio Anton; 36–37, Charles O'Rear/NationalGeographicStock.com; 39, Stuart Armstrong; 40, Alex Grimm/Reuters/Corbis; 40–41, Gregory Manchess/NationalGeographicStock.com; 42, Raymond Gehman/NationalGeographicStock.com; 43, Arthur Max/Associated Press; 44–45, Jay H. Matternes/NationalGeographicStock.com

National Geographic's net proceeds support vital exploration, conservation, research, and education programs.

For more information, please call 1-800-NGS LINE (647-5463) or write to the following address:
National Geographic Society
1145 17th Street N.W.
Washington, D.C. 20036-4688 U.S.A.

Visit us online at nationalgeographic.com/books
For librarians and teachers: ngchildrensbooks.org
More for kids from National Geographic:
kids.nationalgeographic.com

For information about special discounts for bulk purchases, please contact National Geographic Books Special Sales: ngspecsales@ngs.org

For rights or permissions inquiries, please contact National Geographic Books Subsidiary Rights: ngbookrights@ngs.org

Front cover: A photo composite shows Lyuba, a baby mammoth, embedded in ice.

Pages 2–3: Nenets children get a close-up look at Lyuba outside the Shemanovsky Museum in Salekhard, Siberia.

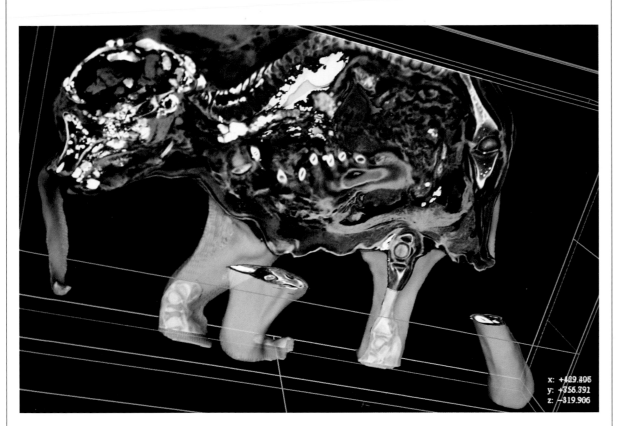

A 3-D medical scan shows researchers what a baby mammoth looks like inside.

x: +429.405
y: +356.391
z: −319.906

CONTENTS

WAKING THE

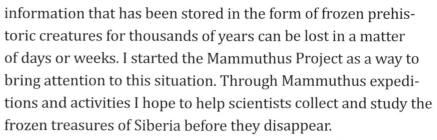

BABY MAMMOTH

I am a mammoth hunter. Not the kind that runs around with a stone spear, but one who hunts for evidence of Ice Age mammals in the tundra of Siberia in northern Russia. I've been to this area many times, and each time I go I learn something new about prehistoric life. Sometimes, if I'm lucky, I hear about a new discovery from my friends, the nomadic reindeer herders known as the Nenets. The May 2007 discovery of Lyuba, the baby woolly mammoth you will read about in this book, was a once-in-a-lifetime experience for me. Never before has such a beautifully preserved mammoth mummy been found.

Over the years, I have seen the remains of many mammoths and other Ice Age animals, such as woolly rhinoceroses and steppe bison, emerge from the permafrost—a deep layer of soil that has been frozen for thousands of years. A collection of these amazing creatures is housed at my expedition base in Khatanga, Siberia, where they are preserved in an ice cave. Scientists from around the world come to Khatanga to study the bones and tusks stored there.

Mammoths provide a great window to the past. They help us understand the evolution of life on Earth at the end of the Ice Age about 10,000 years ago. Unfortunately, Earth's rapidly warming climate is causing the permafrost to melt. As the melting continues, the remains of Ice Age animals such as Lyuba may be lost by exposure to the elements. This means that precious

information that has been stored in the form of frozen prehistoric creatures for thousands of years can be lost in a matter of days or weeks. I started the Mammuthus Project as a way to bring attention to this situation. Through Mammuthus expeditions and activities I hope to help scientists collect and study the frozen treasures of Siberia before they disappear.

I hope as you are reading this book that you will become as

The first largely intact frozen mammoth carcass was discovered in Siberia in 1806.

charmed as I am by this little calf. It is sad that she died so young so long ago, but it makes me happy to think of all of the important things about mammoths and their world that we are learning from her. Thank you, Lyuba.

Bernard Buigues

Bernard Buigues
Director, Mammuthus Project

For Nenets like Yuri Khudi (left) the barren Siberian landscape is home. For Bernard Buigues (right) it is where one goes to "hunt" mammoths.

7

CHAPTER ONE

THE DISCOVERY

Siberia's Nenets are nomadic reindeer herders who have learned to survive winters that can plunge to minus 76°F (-60°C).

The *whoosh* of a sled pulled by reindeer sliced through the stillness of a snowy plain in Siberia. It was May. The tundra was still frozen, but in a few weeks it would begin to thaw. Yuri Khudi and his sons glided along the bank of the Yuribey River. They were taking advantage of the good weather to do some hunting. Perhaps they would spot a game bird or other small animal that would add some variety to a diet of fish and occasional reindeer meat eaten by the Nenets people, who have herded reindeer in Siberia for more than 800 years. The last thing Yuri expected on this outing was that he would make an important scientific discovery.

BABY MAMMOTH: LOST AND FOUND

From a distance, it looked like a dead reindeer lying on a sandbar along the river channel. As Yuri drew closer, however, he thought it looked more like a baby elephant. How could that be? The nearest elephants lived thousands of miles away.

As Yuri and his sons stood around the little body lying on the sandbar, they were shocked by what they had found: a perfectly preserved baby woolly mammoth. It was frozen solid.

These animals disappeared from this part of the world about 11,000 years ago, but mammoth bones and tusks are a relatively common find in Siberia. It's so cold in this Arctic region of Russia that the frozen soil, called permafrost, has acted

This re-creation illustrates what a mammoth carcass would look like as it emerges from the permafrost during a spring thaw.

as a giant freezer, preserving the carcasses of many animals that lived there long ago. As the top layer of permafrost begins to thaw in the spring, the bony remains of mammoths often appear as if they have burst from the frozen ground. But Yuri and his sons had never seen anything like this before—a baby woolly mammoth with all of its flesh in place. It looked like it could have died yesterday. They didn't dare touch it.

The **Nenets'** frozen homeland was once an endless plain of grasses and shrubs called steppe, shared by woolly mammoths and other prehistoric grazing animals.

Nenets keep warm in chums, teepee-like huts made of reindeer hide. Reindeer hide is also often used for clothing, such as boots, parkas, and other outerwear.

LIFE AT
THE "END OF THE EARTH"

YURI AND HIS SONS belong to the ancient Nenets culture, which has inhabited the Yamal Peninsula of Siberia, in northern Russia, for more than 800 years. Yamal means "end of the Earth" in the Nenets language. It's a fitting name for the strip of land that stretches north into the Arctic Ocean to within 1,500 miles (2,400 km) of the North Pole (see map below).

The 40,000 or so Nenets living on the peninsula are nomadic herders who depend on reindeer for survival. They rely on the animal's meat for food and sell it for income. They also use the thick skin to make warm parkas, boots, and large, circular tents called chums. During the nine-month-long winter, the Nenets camp in these tents surrounded by their reindeer. There is no electricity and no telephones, and the only water comes from ice after it is melted. In the spring the Nenets move to pastures where their reindeer can graze on fresh green shoots of grasses and shrubs.

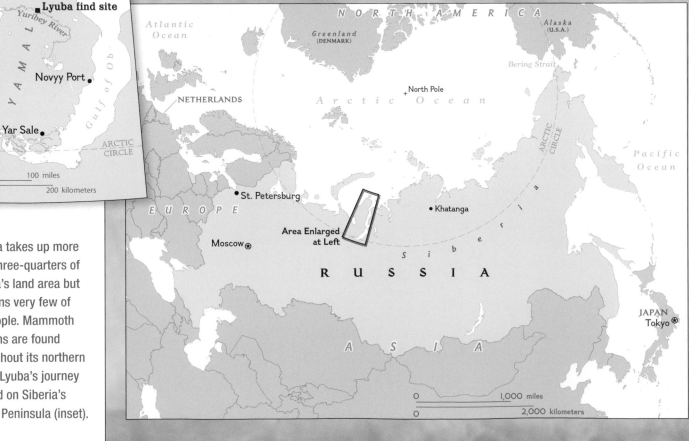

Siberia takes up more than three-quarters of Russia's land area but contains very few of its people. Mammoth remains are found throughout its northern parts. Lyuba's journey started on Siberia's Yamal Peninsula (inset).

Mammoths play a powerful role in Nenets mythology. The story goes that woolly mammoths are giant beasts herded by gods of the underground. If the animals come to the surface and see sunlight, they die. Some Nenets say that mammoths will bring bad luck or even death to the people who touch their remains.

So it was with both fear and respect that Yuri Khudi and his sons looked at the baby mammoth. Uncertain what to do, they left the mammoth exactly where they found it and returned to camp. Yuri decided to seek the advice of Kirill Serotetto, a trusted friend who had lots of experience in the Arctic as an expedition outfitter and knew the value of mammoth bones. To get to Yar Sale, where Serotetto lived, Yuri rode his snow-mobile 90 miles (145 km) to Novyy Port then boarded a helicopter to Yar Sale.

After hearing Yuri's story, Serotetto rushed him to the director of the museum, who notified the local police. Yuri had stumbled onto something big. Hours later, Yuri, Serotetto, and a few policemen were flying toward the place where Yuri had made his discovery. Finally, they landed near the site. The baby mammoth was gone!

Yuri's stomach dropped. He was afraid no one would believe him now. Without a body there was no reason for the police to stick around, so they flew back to Yar Sale. Serotetto stayed behind with his friend to investigate further.

Bernard Buigues uses a laptop to show Yuri and his family photographs taken for a television show about the baby mammoth.

Yuri knew that prehistoric animal remains, especially tusks, were valuable and could fetch a lot of money from fossil collectors or carvers. After making some inquiries, he and Serotetto learned that Yuri's cousin had snatched up the baby mammoth and carted it off on his sled to Novyy Port. There he had traded the valuable find to a store owner in exchange for two years' worth of food and some equipment.

Yuri and Serotetto had to move fast if they were going to save this precious treasure. By the time they arrived in Novyy Port, the little mammoth was propped up in the store and was already causing a stir. People were taking pictures of it with their cell phones. Yuri's heart sank when he saw that stray dogs in town had already gnawed off the baby's tail and most of one ear. But the rest of the body was still in perfect condition. They had to get the mammoth to a safe location fast! Serotetto, with the help of the local police chief, explained the importance of the find to the owner. Finally, after much discussion, he agreed to give up the mammoth.

THE STOLEN MAMMOTH

A Nenets myth as told to Bernard Buigues by a friend of Yuri Khudi

ONCE UPON A TIME there were two gods—the god of Above, and the god of Below. The god of Above had four sons and the god of Below had seven sons.

One day, the two elder sons of the god of Above killed a mammoth that belonged to the god of Below. They ate its flesh for seven days and were well nourished, as there was much meat. They threw the mammoth's head into a lake to hide the fact that they'd killed it.

Soon it happened that the seven sons of the god of Below went to fish in the world of the Above. They also went to see the sons of the god of Above to ask if, by chance, they had seen their mammoth. The sons lied and answered that they had not.

When the seven sons of the god of Below started fishing, however, the lines they cast into the lake snagged the mammoth's head. Having discovered the truth, they returned to the sons of the god of Above and challenged them. They said, "You said you hadn't seen our mammoth, but in fact you ate it!"

When the seven told their father what had happened, the god of Below declared war on the god of Above. His seven sons attacked the god of Above, who called to his sons for help. Thus the war between the Above and the Below started.

Native people of Siberia use most of the mammoth ivory they find to make tool handles, parts for reindeer harnesses, and other useful items. Big tusks like the ones strapped to this reindeer sled are sometimes sold to collectors or carvers.

The two elder sons of the god of Above hid in their father's ear and fired shots at the god of Below, but they could not defeat him. The god of Below then called on his younger sons and asked them to help in the violent war. These sons hid in the mouth of their father, and from there they launched flames of fire at the god of Above.

In the battle that followed, four sons of the god of Below died, leaving only three. The god of Below asked the god of Above for mercy, saying, "You've already killed four of my sons! Let us stop this war. Let's make peace by having our children marry."

So, the two younger sons of the god of Above married the daughter of the god of Below. She brought fire from the world of Below to the world of Above. And this is how the peace was made.

SAFE AND SOUND

At last the baby mammoth was in the hands of museum staff at Yar Sale. Now they needed to find a place where she would be preserved and taken care of. The calf was packed onto a helicopter and flown to the Shemanovsky Museum in Salekhard, a regional capital of Siberia. The director there immediately called Bernard Buigues, a French explorer who had become an expert in mammoths and who had established a center for preserving mammoth remains in the Siberian town of Khatanga. When Bernard heard the exciting news, he offered to organize an international team of experts to study the baby mammoth. The team would include researchers from Russia, the United States, and Japan.

It would take several weeks for the team to assemble in Salekhard. To keep the carcass frozen, it was placed in a freezer. Bernard was the first member to arrive. When he saw the baby mammoth, he was struck by how tiny she was—only 33 inches (84 cm) high and 110 pounds (50 kg) in weight. "I was fascinated by her lifelike expression. Her smiling mouth, her front legs seemingly in motion—it was as if she had been enjoying herself." He couldn't wait for the rest of the team to meet her.

After a brief stay in Yar Sale the baby mammoth was whisked away to Salekhard in a helicopter, as shown in this re-enactment. There, her body would be placed in a freezer to protect it from further damage.

MAMMOTHS, MASTODONS, ELEPHANTS, & MORE

ALL ELEPHANT-LIKE creatures, including mammoths, are part of the order Proboscidea. Today, elephants are the only living proboscideans, and they include just three living species: the African bush elephant, the African forest elephant, and the Asian elephant. In prehistoric times, however, there were many types of proboscideans, including mammoths; mastodons, which lived in North America at the same time as mammoths and looked much like them; gomphotheres, many of which had two upper and two lower tusks; and stegodons, a group of elephant-like animals that ranged from 13 feet (4 m) high at the shoulder to dwarf species that stood only about 4 feet (1 m) high. A proboscidean gets its name from its long, sensitive, muscular nose, called a proboscis, which it uses to grip food. Different groups of proboscideans had different tusk and trunk arrangements, as shown in the art at right. To identify a specific proboscidean, match its number with the number and name on the chart below.

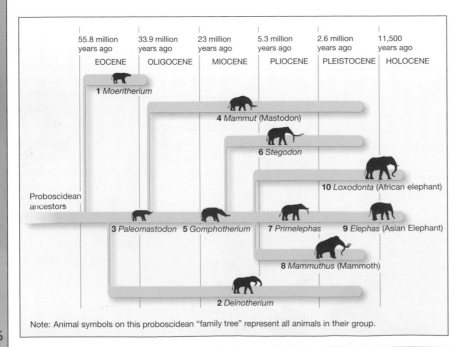

55.8 million years ago	33.9 million years ago	23 million years ago	5.3 million years ago	2.6 million years ago	11,500 years ago
EOCENE	OLIGOCENE	MIOCENE	PLIOCENE	PLEISTOCENE	HOLOCENE

1 *Moeritherium*

4 *Mammut* (Mastodon)

6 *Stegodon*

10 *Loxodonta* (African elephant)

Proboscidean ancestors

3 *Paleomastodon* 5 *Gomphotherium* 7 *Primelephas* 9 *Elephas* (Asian Elephant)

8 *Mammuthus* (Mammoth)

2 *Deinotherium*

Note: Animal symbols on this proboscidean "family tree" represent all animals in their group.

16

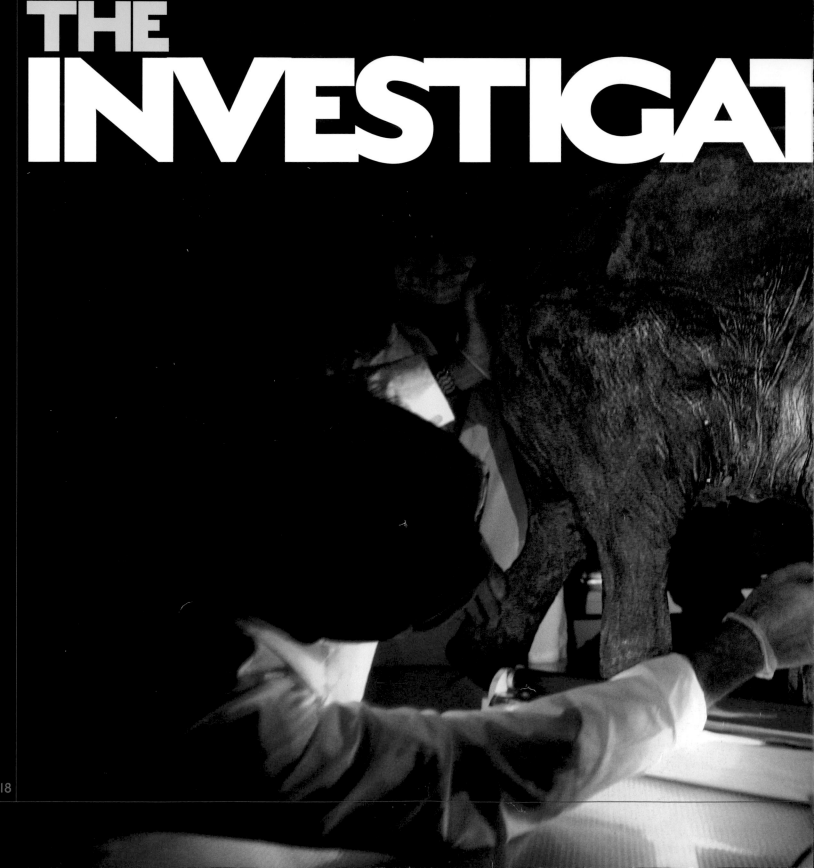

THE INVESTIGAT

ION

Lyuba became the
subject of a series of
intense investigations
that involved a variety
of state-of-the-art
equipment and travel
to several cities.

News of the baby mammoth was starting to spread around the world. Some reports even called her the "world's most valuable discovery." Bernard's team of experts, which included Alexei Tikhonov, vice president of the Zoological Institute in St. Petersburg, Russia, and Dan Fisher, of the University of Michigan, could hardly contain their excitement as they waited to get their first look at the prehistoric creature.

RARE OPPORTUNITY

They stared in amazement as they gazed at the best preserved baby mammoth they had ever seen. She was missing most of her shaggy hair, toenails, and the chewed-off bit of tail and ear, but other than that, she was completely intact. Before the team's arrival, officials at the Shemanovsky Museum had decided to name the little calf Lyuba, after Yuri Khudi's wife. The word, which means "love" in Russian, seemed fitting for this charming visitor from the past.

Everything about Lyuba was a mystery. When did she live? How did she die? What caused the strange dent in her face just above her trunk? And what secrets could she reveal about her prehistoric world? The team would have to draw on their own skills and those of other experts at state-of-the-art research facilities around the world to uncover the truth about Lyuba's life and death.

Lyuba was extremely well preserved, but her stumpy little feet, like the one shown here from the bottom, had lost their toenails, and she had very little hair left on her body.

INVESTIGATION I:
Groningen, Netherlands
MISSION:
Find out when Lyuba lived

Woolly mammoths lived from about 800,000 to 3,700 years ago. But the scientists wanted to know when during that time little Lyuba roamed the plains of Siberia with her mom. So the team took a tissue sample from her body and sent it to a laboratory in the Netherlands.

Woolly mammoths, African elephants, and Asian elephants all evolved in Africa from a common ancestor about six million years ago.

The team got its first look at Lyuba at the museum in Salekhard. She was undamaged except where the dogs in Novyy Port had gnawed off her tail and right ear.

There, experts used radiocarbon dating to find the answer. All living things contain the element carbon. There are different forms of carbon known as isotopes. One isotope of carbon is carbon-14. Over time it changes to nitrogen-14 (see page 33). The age of a specimen can be determined by finding out how much of the carbon-14 has changed to nitrogen-14. The results showed that Lyuba lived 42,000 years ago.

INVESTIGATION 2:
Tokyo, Japan
MISSION:
Look inside Lyuba

The scientists were anxious to see if the inside of Lyuba's body was as well preserved as the outside. This would require a special 3-D x-ray machine called a CT scanner. Naoki Suzuki, another member of Bernard's team, had one in his laboratory in Japan. The team knew that transporting the mammoth that far would be risky. Lyuba had to stay frozen or she would start to decompose. Keeping her frozen and clean would also help protect her body from mold, bacteria, and other unwanted organisms. Plus it would ensure that any ancient bacteria or viruses she might be carrying didn't endanger her human handlers. So the scientists came up with an elaborate plan.

In Japan Lyuba was placed in a specially built container and carried through sterile, plastic tunnels to the research laboratory.

They packed the baby mammoth in a sealed plastic bag, placed her on top of bags of dry ice in an insulated box, and loaded her onto an airplane. Her arrival at Tokyo's Jikei University School of Medicine was like something out of a science-fiction movie. The scientists who greeted her looked like astronauts, wearing face masks and covered from head to toe in sterile suits.

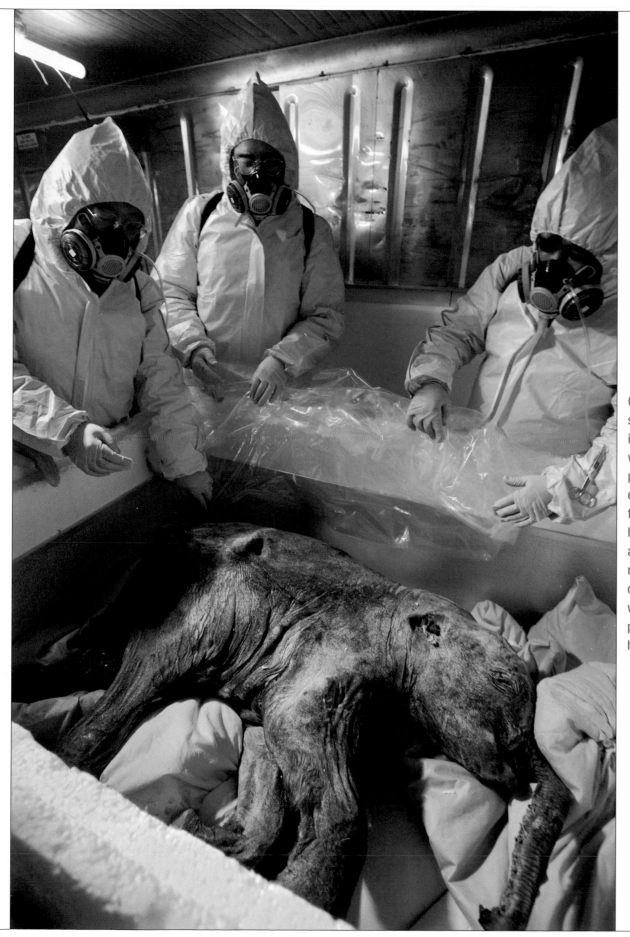

Officials at the university laboratory in Tokyo insisted the scientists wear plastic suits as protection against any dangerous microbes from the past that might have been preserved along with Lyuba. The masks would provide oxygen if carbon dioxide were released from the packs of dry ice lining her container.

Naoki Suzuki studies a 3-D model of Lyuba that allowed researchers to see inside her body.

Bernard's team of experts opened the insulated box and peered anxiously inside. Much to their relief, Lyuba was still frozen and had survived the journey undamaged. They carefully transferred the baby mammoth to a special container that would fit inside the CT scanner, lifted it out of the van, and carried it through a clear plastic tunnel straight into Suzuki's state-of-the-art laboratory.

The team wasted no time in placing the container holding Lyuba on a sliding platform that would move it through the CT scanner. This machine would create

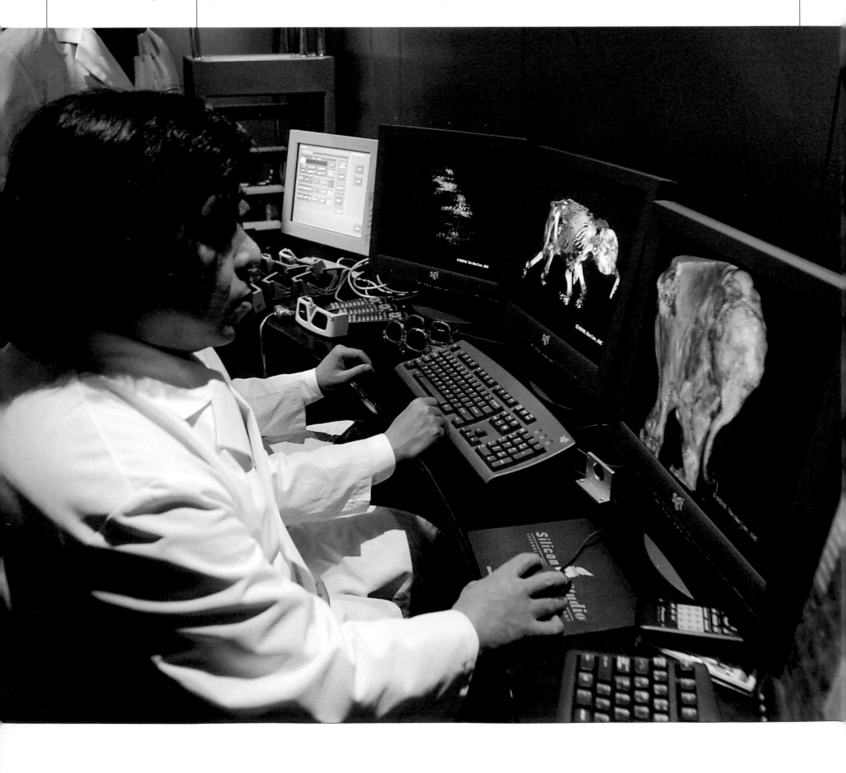

While in Japan Lyuba was placed on public display in a vault-like, refrigerated container.

multiple x-ray images of Lyuba that could be put together by a computer to show the inside of her body in 3-D. The images show different densities of bone, organ, and other tissue. This way the scientists could see into Lyuba without cutting into her body.

The scans showed what the scientists hoped they would: Lyuba was almost as well preserved inside as she was outside. Her heart, stomach, intestines, and lungs were all about where they should be. But the scans also showed that something was wrong in Lyuba's trunk and throat. These passageways, which should have been clear so that she could breathe, were filled with a dense substance. The researchers were excited. Had they discovered a clue to what had caused Lyuba's death?

Suzuki and Fisher saw some other mysterious things on Lyuba's CT scans. Some areas appeared to be covered with some sort of fine-grained material, and small areas inside some of her bones showed up as bright spots on the scans. The only way to find out what these things were and what was blocking the calf's trunk and air passages was to go inside Lyuba's body, using some of the same tools a surgeon does when operating on a patient. But this was a job for another lab.

INVESTIGATION 3:
St. Petersburg, Russia
MISSION:
Perform a mammoth autopsy

Before long Lyuba was back on an airplane in her traveling freezer and on the way to a genetics laboratory in St. Petersburg, Russia. Bernard, Fisher, and Suzuki joined paleontologist Alexei Tikhonov at the laboratory a few months later. Together they would carefully open up Lyuba's body. For them, it would be like opening a treasure chest.

They didn't know what they would find, but expectations were high that the examination would not only tell them about Lyuba's life and cause of death, it would also open up a window into life on Earth 42,000 years ago.

The autopsy would take three days. Once again they put on sterile outfits and surgical masks and began their examination. Prehistoric secrets lay just under their fingertips. Their challenge? To cut Lyuba open and sew her back up with as little damage as possible. That way Lyuba would be preserved for studies by other scientists and future generations.

HEALTHY FAT

The scientists' first task was to inspect the hump on the back of Lyuba's neck. The mammoth experts wondered if the creatures stored extra fat in their humps to help them survive long, cold winters, and, if so, how long it took to build up a supply. Based on the amount of fat they found in a pencil-thin sample from Lyuba's hump, it appeared that well-fed baby mammoths born in late winter or early spring were rapidly building fat reserves for the following fall and winter.

Researchers also looked into Lyuba's ears for mites—tiny bugs that live in the ears of many modern mammals—and other microscopic creatures that might have existed in Lyuba's prehistoric environment.

Most studies show that the woolly mammoth's closest living relative is the Asian elephant.

DNA, DUST, & BRIGHT SPOTS

They snipped off little bits of woolly hair from Lyuba's legs. The hair, if it had not been too damaged over time, might still contain some DNA, the material that contains hereditary information about an organism. Within the DNA researchers might be able to find genes, the specific genetic material that makes a mammoth a mammoth and a mouse a mouse. With a great deal of luck scientists might be able to piece together genes from many strands of DNA to make a complete genetic map called a genome.

Suzuki placed an endoscope—a narrow tube with a camera lens on the end—into a small hole he made in Lyuba's side and guided it through her insides by looking at a computer monitor. The team could see that the fine-grained substance revealed by the CT scan was blue. Fisher recognized it as vivianite, a mineral produced in part from the mineral phosphate, which occurs naturally in bones and soft tissue. Earlier the scientists

The team gets a look into Lyuba's body as Suzuki inserts an endoscope into a small hole in her side.

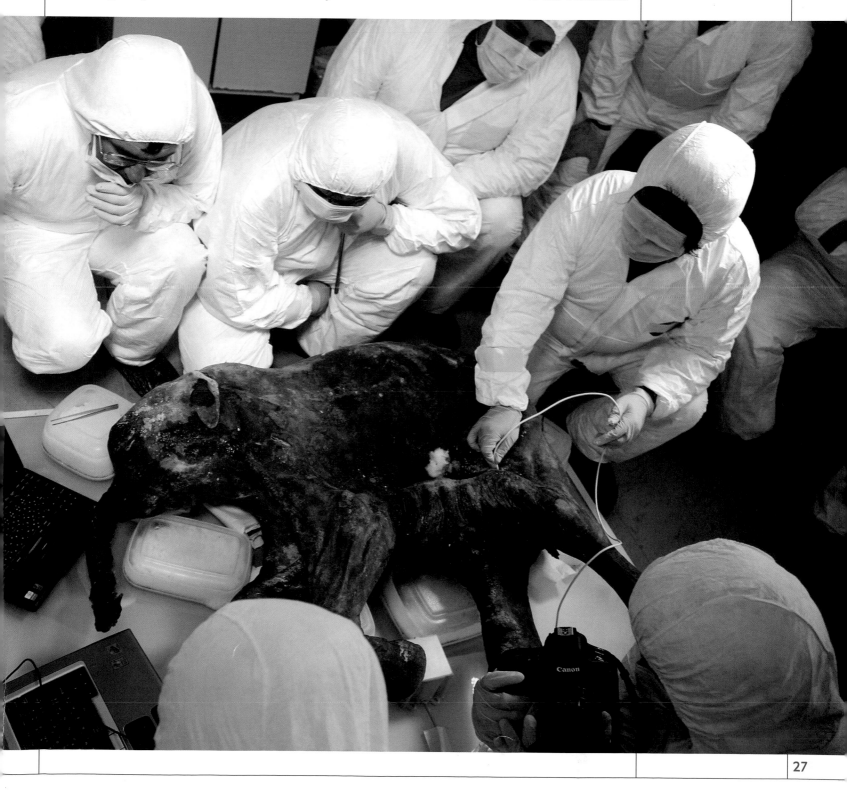

27

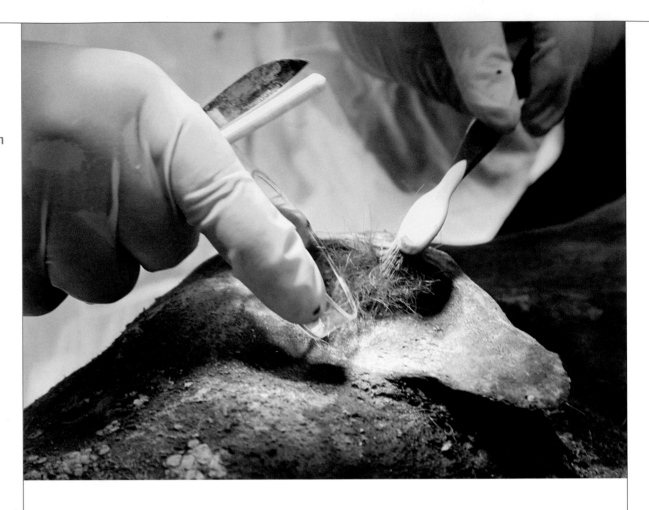

A researcher uses a toothbrush to collect mites and other tiny organisms that might have been preserved in Lyuba's ear.

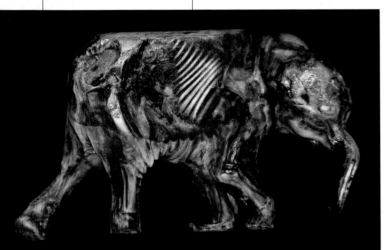

White areas on the CT scan are bones and other dense substances. This image shows that something is blocking part of her trunk.

had found vivianite on her skin, especially on the side that had rested on the sandbar. They suspected that the same mineral caused the bright spots in some of Lyuba's bones, but why was there so much of it inside her body?

TRUNK TRAUMA

Further dissection and probing with an endoscope revealed that mud was blocking Lyuba's trunk and air passages. In all likelihood the baby mammoth had suffocated in thick muck as it plugged her air passages before reaching her lungs. The mud was probably the source of the layer of vivianite in her body, and it also might help explain the odd dent in her face. When Lyuba sucked mud into her trunk, she tried to dislodge it by inhaling sharply, but this pulled the mud straight back into the air passages near her lungs and blocked them. As the mud was sucked out of her trunk into her air passages, a vacuum was created. This collapsed the soft tissue of her trunk and created the dent. With some of their biggest questions already answered, the team was anxious to see what other mysteries the autopsy would solve.

This artist's depiction shows little Lyuba struggling for air while her mother and other mammoths in the group look on helplessly. Scientists suggest she drowned or suffocated in mud.

29

SEALED IN TIME

Lyuba's 42,000-year journey to our time began when she suffocated in mud or drowned in water and was covered over.

1. Microbes (white arrows) in Lyuba's wet grave penetrated her body and stopped her corpse from decaying.

RIVER

BANK

2. Soon Lyuba's moist environment became locked in a layer of permanently frozen soil called permafrost.

NEW SEDIMENT

PERMAFROST

3. Erosion caused by the rushing waters of a spring ice melt freed Lyuba from her frozen tomb and washed her downriver where Yuri discovered her.

RIVER

LAST MEAL

Fisher made a square cut in Lyuba's side so he could reach her intestines to see what she had been eating. Amazingly, they still contained the 42,000-year-old remains of her last meal. The researchers found traces of the mother's milk that Lyuba had nursed on the day she died. They also discovered that the calf had been eating her mother's dung—something that baby elephants do. Mother elephants pass bacteria to their calves through their dung. These help the babies digest plants once they stop nursing. It was exciting to find this link between mammoth and elephant behavior, but there was more. The dung would also reveal what kinds of plants Lyuba's mom had been eating, which could lead to new information about the vegetation that existed in Siberia tens of thousands of years ago.

TELLTALE SMELL

Cutting into Lyuba's slightly thawed body to get samples had released a distinct, sour odor that reminded Fisher of an experiment he had made several years earlier. From his studies of mammoth finds in North America he noticed that their bones were often discovered in places once covered by water. Had ancient hunters stored mammoth carcasses in ponds? To see if this method of food storage would work, he sank large chunks of raw horse meat in water for several months. When he tasted the meat, he found that it was still edible. Microbes had prevented decay and, in the process, had produced a sour smell—the same odor coming from Lyuba! Fisher realized that Lyuba had been pickled by the microbes in the wet environment that surrounded her after she died. This had prevented her from rotting and likely had made her body smell unappetizing to scavengers.

The autopsy had solved many mysteries, but still unknown was Lyuba's age when she died. Fisher knew where to find the answer—in her tusks and teeth. He carefully extracted one of her tiny milk tusks and a cheek tooth, or premolar, to take back to his lab in the United States.

Tusks start growing in a baby mammoth's mouth before it is born. These tusks are replaced by permanent tusks that keep growing until the day the animal dies. They grow a little longer every day as a new microscopic layer of dentin is added. Dentin is what makes up most of the tusk. By cutting Lyuba's tusk in half, Fisher could count the layers of dentin like the growth rings in a tree trunk. But how would he know where to start counting? Earlier studies of another baby mammoth showed that the stress of birth is recorded in the tusk as a darker layer of dentin. The same thing has been observed in some other animals, including humans. This marks the first day of life. Fisher found a similar marker in Lyuba's tusk. He counted 32 layers, confirming that Lyuba was 32 days old when she died.

CHEMICAL CLUES

Lyuba's tiny milk tusk promises to reveal new information about how mammoth biology compares with that of living elephants.

Tusks grow by adding layers of dentin every day. These layers are microscopic, but this cross section of a mammoth tusk shows the ringlike pattern of that growth.

Much of what we know about mammoths and their environment has come from their tusks. Hidden in the dentin layers are chemical traces of the food they ate. By studying the makeup of tooth material, scientists can determine what food sources were available at the time and how well the animal was doing in its environment. Combining this sort of detailed information about mammoths with findings about other prehistoric animals, plants, and climate makes it possible for Fisher and other scientists to reconstruct the Ice Age world and suggest reasons for the mammoths' extinction.

HOW DO WE KNOW HOW OLD THINGS ARE?

Australopithecus afarensis
4 to 3 million years ago
3 feet (1 m) to 5 feet (1.5 m) tall

ONE OF THE FIRST QUESTIONS

researchers who study prehistoric life ask is, "How old is it?" Scientists now have many ways to answer that question. Accurate ages can be found by looking at the sequence of geological layers, flip-flops in the magnetism of Earth's Poles that are recorded in rocks, and at the decay of radioactive particles trapped in rocks or even in animal or plant tissue. Life on Earth is more than 3.5 billion years old. Compared to the time of dinosaurs, Lyuba lived just moments ago.

ORIGIN OF HUMANS
7 to 6 million years ago

EARLIEST ELEPHANT-LIKE ANIMALS
55 million years ago

FIRST DINOSAURS
240 million years ago

Tyrannosaurus rex
67 million years ago
42 feet (12.8 m) long

Platybelodon
15 million years ago
10 feet (3 m) tall

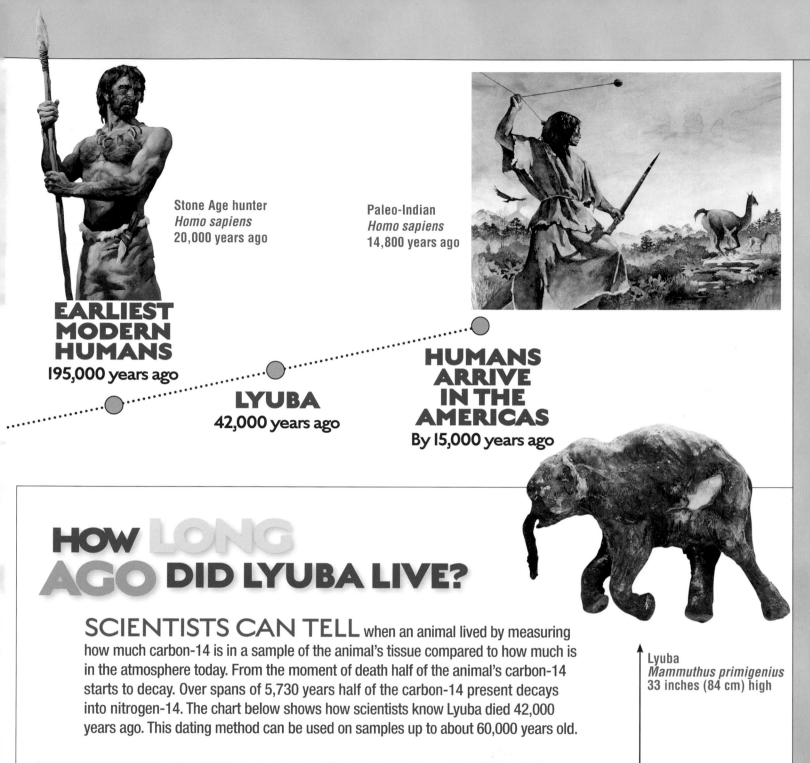

Stone Age hunter
Homo sapiens
20,000 years ago

Paleo-Indian
Homo sapiens
14,800 years ago

EARLIEST MODERN HUMANS
195,000 years ago

LYUBA
42,000 years ago

HUMANS ARRIVE IN THE AMERICAS
By 15,000 years ago

HOW LONG AGO DID LYUBA LIVE?

SCIENTISTS CAN TELL when an animal lived by measuring how much carbon-14 is in a sample of the animal's tissue compared to how much is in the atmosphere today. From the moment of death half of the animal's carbon-14 starts to decay. Over spans of 5,730 years half of the carbon-14 present decays into nitrogen-14. The chart below shows how scientists know Lyuba died 42,000 years ago. This dating method can be used on samples up to about 60,000 years old.

Lyuba
Mammuthus primigenius
33 inches (84 cm) high

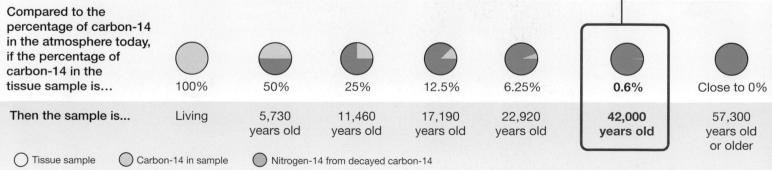

Compared to the percentage of carbon-14 in the atmosphere today, if the percentage of carbon-14 in the tissue sample is...	100%	50%	25%	12.5%	6.25%	0.6%	Close to 0%
Then the sample is...	Living	5,730 years old	11,460 years old	17,190 years old	22,920 years old	**42,000 years old**	57,300 years old or older

○ Tissue sample   ● Carbon-14 in sample   ● Nitrogen-14 from decayed carbon-14

Note: The red outline highlights Lyuba and indicates a break in time for the chart.

Woolly mammoths, with their bulk and huge appetites, played an important role in shaping their environment, called the mammoth steppe.

CHAPTER THREE

LYUBA'S WORLD

T he landscape of the Yamal Peninsula of Siberia, where Lyuba was discovered, looked completely different when the baby mammoth lived there 42,000 years ago. Lush grasslands called steppe flourished where icy tundra exists today. It teemed with millions of animals—mammoths, reindeer, muskoxen, steppe bison, and a variety of smaller creatures. During the spring, soon after Lyuba and all baby mammoths were born, the area was a sea of flowing green grasses with rivers, bogs, and lakes dotting the landscape.

SURVIVING THE STEPPE

For mammoths and other plant-eating animals the steppe was an ideal place to breed and raise their young. There was plenty of food and water, and large family groups provided safety in numbers. But danger always lurked nearby. Anywhere mammoths lived, carnivores, such as cave lions, gray wolves, brown bears, hyenas, and wolverines were not far away. If Lyuba had strayed too far from the safety of her mother's side, she would have been easy prey.

Lyuba was so young that she survived solely on her mother's milk. But older members of her family group would have feasted on grasses, shrubs, and grasslike plants called sedges during the short summer growing season. But young and old alike had to prepare for the long, cold winters. Building up a store of fat, just as Lyuba did in her little hump, might make the difference between life and death.

Lyuba's hair would have been growing longer. Pressing up against her mother's big, hairy body could provide some protection from the cold winds that would come with winter, but the baby would need a

When spring comes to Siberia's Yamal Peninsula (below), ice and snow melt quickly, revealing a pattern of rivers and bogs similar to what might have existed on parts of the mammoth steppe.

The crowd of animals on the mammoth steppe can be compared to that on the Serengeti in East Africa today.

The mammoth steppe burst with green in late spring much like the Siberian steppe (below) does today. Almost all mammoth steppe plants still grow on the Yamal Peninsula and other areas.

coat of her own. Like all woolly mammoths, she would have an undercoat of fine yellowish brown wool to keep her body warm and dry, and an outer layer of shaggy hair. This would have been either dark brown, rusty red, or even blonde and would have provided extra protection by trapping air between the two layers of fur.

Other parts of a mammoth's anatomy helped the animals survive in a cold environment. Unlike today's elephants, which have large ears that they can flap to cool off, woolly mammoths had tiny ears. The small size of their ears plus the fact that they were covered with hair helped keep heat inside their bodies.

Woolly mammoths had an overall shorter, stockier build than other mammoths. This meant that less of their bodies was exposed to cold air. And layers of fat under their skin helped keep them warm. Woolly mammoth tusks were huge compared to their stocky bodies. The animals may have used them to sweep aside snow so they could munch on the edible plants underneath.

Adult males probably lived separately from females and their young except during mating season, when large males would come back to the family group. Male mammoths likely used their huge, spiral-shaped tusks—which were as

> ## A key to mammoth survival was having blood that could carry oxygen to cells at very low temperatures.

Modern human hunters with Stone Age technology coexisted with woolly mammoths for tens of thousands of years in Europe and Asia before the animals became extinct there. In North America the time between the arrival of hunters and the time that mammoths became extinct was much shorter.

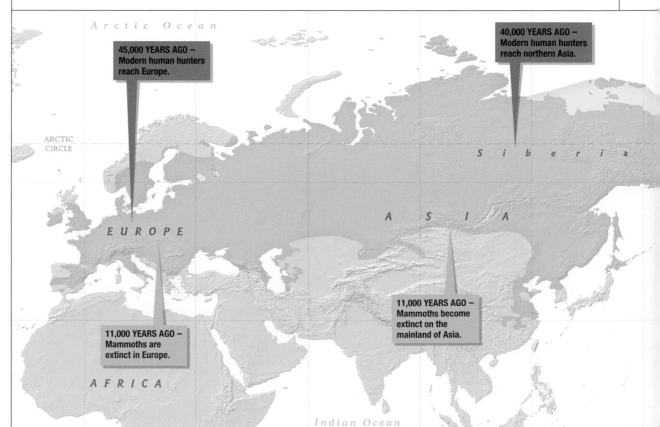

45,000 YEARS AGO – Modern human hunters reach Europe.

40,000 YEARS AGO – Modern human hunters reach northern Asia.

11,000 YEARS AGO – Mammoths are extinct in Europe.

11,000 YEARS AGO – Mammoths become extinct on the mainland of Asia.

thick as tree trunks and sometimes grew to more than 14 feet (4 m) long—to battle other males and attract females.

WHY DID MAMMOTHS DISAPPEAR?

These yearly rituals played out for thousands of years on the mammoth steppe, which once stretched across land-masses in the Northern Hemisphere from the British Isles to North America. But this world would not last forever. When tiny Lyuba was born 42,000 years ago, millions of mammoths roamed Earth's northern grasslands. By 10,000 years ago, mammoths had disappeared from all but the most remote areas of Siberia and a few isolated islands off its coast. They had completely vanished by 3,700 years ago. What caused them to become extinct so quickly is still a mystery. There are several theories, but the two most likely involve climate change and hunting.

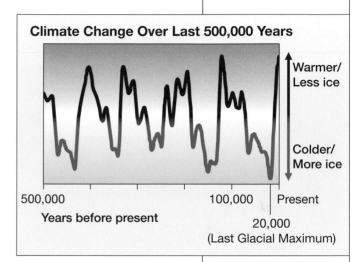

CLIMATE CHAOS—One of Earth's coldest climates in the last million years occurred about 20,000 years ago. During this time, known as the Last Glacial Maximum, a polar

Woolly mammoths survived many ups and downs of climate over hundreds of thousands of years. They were extinct in most places 8,000 to 15,000 years after the rapid thawing of the Last Glacial Maximum.

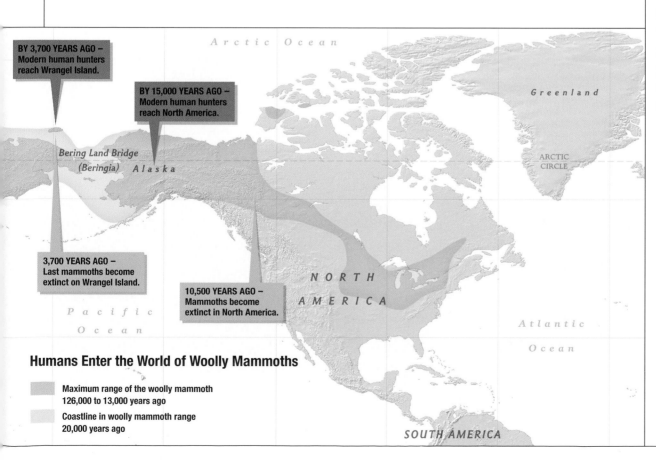

BY 3,700 YEARS AGO – Modern human hunters reach Wrangel Island.

BY 15,000 YEARS AGO – Modern human hunters reach North America.

3,700 YEARS AGO – Last mammoths become extinct on Wrangel Island.

10,500 YEARS AGO – Mammoths become extinct in North America.

Bering Land Bridge (Beringia)   Alaska

Arctic Ocean

Greenland

ARCTIC CIRCLE

NORTH AMERICA

Pacific Ocean

Atlantic Ocean

SOUTH AMERICA

Humans Enter the World of Woolly Mammoths

Maximum range of the woolly mammoth
126,000 to 13,000 years ago

Coastline in woolly mammoth range
20,000 years ago

ice cap stretched from the North Pole all the way down to the Great Lakes of North America. Many places in Europe and Asia that seldom see snow today were covered with deep, icy glaciers. Within another 10,000 years—a short time in geological history—Earth was warm like it is today. Such rapid climate change would have had a dramatic impact on Earth's ecosystems. The mammoths and the environment that sustained them may not have survived these sudden changes. But some scientists think climate change may have been only one part of the story or may not have been part of the extinction process at all.

HUNTED TO EXTINCTION—When modern humans first reached the northern parts of Europe and Asia about 45,000 years ago, mammoths were still thriving. These Stone Age hunter-gatherers used tools made of stone and survived by hunting animals and collecting edible plants as they moved from place to place.

Stone Age campsites unearthed in Europe and Asia are littered with mammoth bones as well as stone tools and weapons. By studying evidence from such sites, scientists have learned that these Ice Age people

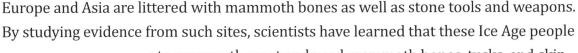

ate mammoth meat and used mammoth bones, tusks, and skin for tools, clothes, and shelter. They even used the dung for fuel and to keep warm. Mammoths were important to their survival.

These humans may have followed the mammoths into North America, crossing the Bering Land Bridge that connected Siberia and Alaska at that time (see map pages 38–39). The area, now called the Bering Strait, is underwater today, but during the Ice Age things were different. So much of the world's water was locked up in the polar ice cap and glaciers that sea levels dropped enough to expose land usually covered by water.

This mammoth figurine, perhaps a pendant, shows that Stone Age people used mammoth bones and ivory to make more than tools, needles, and other practical things.

The woolly mammoth was the last surviving mammoth species to walk on Earth.

Some researchers think Stone Age people rarely hunted mammoths because they were so difficult to kill. Instead, as shown here, they scavenged dead ones for meat, hide, and ivory.

Did an object from space explode in the atmosphere, causing extensive wildfires and a sudden cooling 12,800 years ago? Some researchers think so. They suggest this event may have contributed to the extinction of woolly mammoths.

By 12,800 years ago the mammoth population in North America was on the brink of becoming extinct.

The last known mammoths on Earth lived on Wrangel Island, off the northern coast of Siberia, about 3,700 years ago. Scientists have found evidence indicating that this is the same time period that humans arrived on the island. But there is no evidence to show that humans were killing mammoths in large enough numbers to cause their extinction. That is why many scientists think it was a combination of climate change and hunting that caused mammoths to disappear. But since no one knows for sure, some researchers have looked for other explanations.

DEADLY DISEASE—Animals living in a world populated by humans—or humans themselves—may have brought diseases with them when they crossed the Bering Land Bridge from Asia. This could have caused a deadly epidemic among mammoths already in North America. But some researchers object to this idea. They point out that several animals in a population usually have immunities that would allow them to survive an epidemic.

EXTRATERRESTRIAL EXPLOSION—Some researchers suggest that a large object from outer space, possibly a meteoroid or comet, exploded in the atmosphere over North America around 12,900 years ago. Such an event could have triggered a sudden cool period that lasted for the next 1,300 years, disrupting environments, and perhaps driving many species to extinction. They argue that a dark layer of earth found at archaeological sites comes from ash left by widespread fires caused by the explosion. They also say that tiny diamonds found in microscopic particles in that layer could only have come from outer space. Opponents say that such particles are always raining down on Earth from space and that the scorched earth came from normally occurring forest fires.

Could a perfectly preserved baby woolly mammoth help answer one of the biggest mysteries on Earth: Why did mammoths become extinct? Since she lived well before the extinction, she probably can't shed much light on that mystery, but thanks to new technology, mammoth mummies might be able to help in another way. Their DNA could provide scientists with what they need to re-create this Ice Age giant.

WILL MAMMOTHS LIVE AGAIN?

Some say yes. Hendrik Poinar, an expert on ancient DNA, goes so far as to say that it is just a matter of working out the details. Researchers have made clones of sheep, pigs, and many other animals, and one day they could clone a mammoth. By stitching together tiny pieces of ancient DNA that come from the tissue of well-preserved mammoths such as Lyuba, scientists hope to one day re-create a complete mammoth genome. Similar to the way animals are cloned today, the re-created mammoth DNA could replace elephant DNA in an elephant egg. If the egg grew properly, the mother elephant would give birth to a baby mammoth.

Today researchers are also trying to re-create the mammoth steppe. They are introducing

Muskoxen are among the large animals that survived the Ice Age. Researchers hope young muskoxen, like the ones shown here, will help in efforts to re-create a small version of the mammoth steppe.

large animals, such as reindeer and muskoxen, to a park in Siberia. The hope is that over time these big animals, by keeping plants cropped low and fertilizing the soil, will have the same impact that mammoths and other large Ice Age animals had on their environment. If all goes according to plan, the park could one day welcome home a baby mammoth that would roam the steppe just as Lyuba did many thousands of years ago.

RE-CREATING A VANISHED WORLD

ICE AGE ANIMALS ROAM this re-created scene of life on the grassy, summer tundra in Alaska more than five hundred centuries ago. Back then the area was part of the mammoth steppe. As temperatures dropped and the ice advanced over the mountains and as they encountered human hunters, many animals became extinct. Those that disappeared are marked with a red dot. Unmarked animals or close relatives still survive either in Alaska or in Asia. If scientists succeed in cloning Ice Age animals and re-creating their habitat, we won't need a painting to show us what life on the mammoth steppe looked like. We will be able to see it with our own eyes.

GROUND SLOTH

HUMANS

MOOSE

LARGE-HORNED BISON

GREAT NORTH AMERICAN SHORT-FACED BEAR

MUSKOXEN

LYNX

WOLF

ARCTIC FOX

ALASKA TUNDRA HARE

DALL SHEEP

WOOLLY MAMMOTH

PREHISTORIC CAMEL

MASTODON

WAPITI

YAK

STAG-MOOSE

WOLVERINE

GRIZZLY BEAR

SABER-TOOTHED CAT

LIONLIKE CAT

RED FOX

ARCTIC HORSE

SAIGA ANTELOPE

BADGER

ARCTIC GROUND SQUIRREL

BROWN LEMMING

RESOURCES

Further reading:

Fagan, Brian. *The Complete Ice Age: How Climate Change Shaped the World*. Thames and Hudson, 2009.

Gore, Rick. "The Dawn of Humans: People Like Us." *National Geographic* (July 2000), 90–117.

Kurten, Björn. *Dance of the Tiger: A Novel of the Ice Age.* University of California Press, 1995.

Lister, Adrian, and Paul Bahn. *Mammoths: Giants of the Ice Age.* University of California Press, 2009.

Martin, Paul. *Twilight of the Mammoths: Ice Age Extinctions and the Rewilding of America.* University of California Press, 2007.

Meltzer, David. *First Peoples in a New World: Colonizing Ice Age America*. University of California Press, 2010.

Montaigne, Fen. "Nenets: Surviving on the Siberian Tundra." *National Geographic* (March 1998), 120–137.

Mueller, Tom. "Ice Baby: Secrets of a Frozen Mammoth." *National Geographic* (May 2009), 30–51.

Parfit, Michael. "Dawn of Humans: Hunt for the First Americans." *National Geographic* (December 2000), 40–67.

Online resources:

Understanding Evolution
evolution.berkeley.edu/

The Paleontology Portal
paleoportal.org/

Smithsonian Human Origins Initiative
humanorigins.si.edu/

National Oceanic and Atmospheric Administration Climate Timeline
ncdc.noaa.gov/paleo/ctl/100k.html

National Oceanic and Atmospheric Administration paleoclimatology slide set
msu.edu/user/tuckeys1/education/ PROMSE_06/Supplemental%20 Material/Glaciation%20notes. pdf?pagewanted=all

National Oceanic and Atmospheric Administration Educational Outreach–Glaciation
ncdc.noaa.gov/paleo/glaciation.html

Geological Society of America geologic time scale
geosociety.org/science/timescale/

autopsy an examination of a dead body to figure out its state of health at the time of death and, if possible, the cause of death

climate all weather conditions for a given location over a period of time

clone (cloning) an individual organism genetically identical to another one because it was grown from a single cell or a cell nucleus from the other "parent" organism

dentin a hard, dense material found in teeth, usually under the enamel, which continues to grow throughout life

DNA stands for **d**eoxyribo**n**ucleic **a**cid, an inheritable molecule that contains the genetic instructions for development, growth, and other functions of living organisms

ecosystem a community of organisms and the environment with which they interact

environment all of the conditions that surround and influence an organism

genes genetic information within DNA composed of specific sections of DNA and producing specific results. Genes can be very short or very long. They can work alone or in tandem with other genes to produce results, which can range from governing metabolism to generating eye color. Some genes are associated with disease. Genes are passed on from one organism to another through inheritance.

genetics the study of the structure, functions, and inheritance of genes and the resulting variation in organisms

genome the complete set of an organism's inherited genetic instructions, such as appear in DNA

habitat the natural environment in which an animal or plant is usually found or prefers to exist

Ice Age a cold period during which glaciers advance and ice at the poles may expand. Much of Earth's history is made up of glacial periods, or ice ages, and interglacials, or warm periods. The term Ice Age, when capitalized, refers to the entire Pleistocene epoch (2.6 million to about 11,500 years ago) during which there were several major glaciations and interglacials. The last glacial period of the Pleistocene lasted from 100,000 to 10,000 years ago.

isotopes variations within atoms of an element, such as carbon, representing different numbers of neutrons in the nucleus

Last Glacial Maximum the point at which the glacial advance of an ice age reaches its maximum extent. The Last Glacial Maximum, when capitalized, refers to this event in the Pleistocene, which occurred 20,000 years ago.

mammoth steppe a largely treeless area of vegetation consisting of sedges and grasses that existed during the Pleistocene as part of an ecosystem dominated by large herbivores, such as mammoths and steppe bison

microbes microscopic organisms, such as bacteria

microorganisms organisms of microscopic size, such as bacteria

milk tusks precursors of tusks that grow unerupted in an elephant from gestation until a short time after birth

order a grouping scientists use to classify organisms. A class, such as Mammalia (mammals) is made up of orders. An order, such as Proboscidea, is made up of families, such as Mammutidae (extinct mastodons), and Elephantidae (includes extinct mammoths and living elephants).

Paleo-Indian the first people who entered and inhabited the Americas

Paleolithic (see Stone Age)

permafrost soil that remains frozen year-round. Permafrost is usually found in northern latitudes.

prehistoric before written records

radioactive a substance that, because of its instability, loses energy from the nucleus of its atoms by emitting particles. The process of losing such particles is called radioactive decay. Carbon-14 is considered a radioactive isotope of carbon.

radiocarbon dating a method of dating organic material, such as animal or plant tissue, by measuring the percentage of carbon-14 in the sample. All living things absorb this isotope of carbon from the atmosphere, along with other isotopes of carbon. Carbon-14 is unstable. Because the rate of radioactive decay of carbon-14 is known, the percentage of carbon present in a sample can be used to tell how long ago an organism stopped absorbing carbon-14—in other words, when it died.

species one of the basic units of classification for organisms. The woolly mammoth, for example, is a species of mammoth. Members of a species can interbreed and produce fertile offspring of their own species.

steppe relatively flat, mostly treeless, temperate grasslands that stretch across much of central Europe and central Asia

Stone Age a period of time during which humans and human ancestors used stone tools. Since stone tools have been used for more than 2.6 million years, scientists break the Stone Age, also known as the Paleolithic, into and early, middle, and late phase. Woolly mammoths interacted with humans from the middle Stone Age, during which time Neandertals lived, and the late Stone Age. Only modern humans are associated with the late Stone Age.

tundra a biological and physical region at high latitudes and elevations that is characterized by cold temperatures, low vegetation, extensive permafrost and waterlogged soils, and a short growing season

GLOSSARY

INDEX

Illustrations are indicated by **boldface**.

3-D model 5, **5**, 24, **24**, 25

The following sub-entries are part of the "Mammoths, when she lived" column:

size 15, 33, **33**
trunk 25, 28, **28**
tusks 31, **31**
when she lived 20, 22, 33, 36, 39